A Bustle & Sew Publication

Copyright © Bustle & Sew Limited 2013

The right of Helen Dickson to be identified as the author of this work has been asserted in accordance with the Copyright, Designs and Patents Act 1988.

All rights reserved. No part of this publication may be reproduced, stored in a retrieval system or transmitted in any form, or by any means, without the prior written permission of the author, nor be otherwise circulated in any form of binding or cover other than that in which it is published and without a similar condition being imposed on the subsequent purchaser.

Every effort has been made to ensure that all the information in this book is accurate. However, due to differing conditions, tools and individual skills, the publisher cannot be responsible for any injuries, losses and other damages that may result from the use of the information in this book.

First published 2013 by:
Bustle & Sew
Coombe Leigh
Chillington
Kingsbridge
Devon TQ7 2LE
UK

www.bustleandsew.com

With thanks to my friend Jacqui for her beautiful illustrations

Contents

Introduction	Page 5
Getting Started	Page 6
The Patterns:	
Pin Cushion Mice	Page 10
Two French Hens	Page 12
A Muddle of Bunnies	Page 14
Flying Pigs	Page 18
Hodge & Podge	Page 21
Fuzzy and his Carrot	Page 24
Swan Softie	Page 26
Mounted Deer Head	Page 29
Sidney	Page 33
Brave Aviator Mouse	Page 36
Little Giraffe	Page 39
Felt Fox Head	Page 42
Templates	Page 47

Introduction

You don't need to be an expert stitcher to sew an endearing little softie. The materials used in softie-making are very easy to work with and can disguise a multitude of sins. And don't forget, the odd wonky stitch or slightly lop-sided expression will (up to a point) only add to the unique handmade quality of your creations. It is important though, to make space for yourself to work - whether that's simply clearing the kitchen table after your family has eaten or, if you're very lucky, making space in your workroom. Softies don't need a lot of complicated equipment, and many can be made in just an evening or two, so you don't need too much room or lots of expensive tools.

If your softie is intended for a child, then do bear in mind their age. Don't use any buttons, trims or small pieces that may become detached when creating for a child below the age of three as these could be a choking hazard. Some of the softies in this book use wires or the bases are weighted with small pebbles or polybeads and these softies should not be regarded as toys for very young children. You should also keep in mind whether or not the softie is likely to be washed frequently as this will affect your choice of fabric and stitching techniques.

You don't need a huge stash of fabric either, all the projects in this little book use very little fabric and are very economical to create. But do remember that cheap materials will not make an attractive, long-lasting softie. An old piece of good quality material will make a far nicer softie than new, poor quality fabric bought especially for the project.

This book includes a selection of Bustle & Sew softie patterns ranging from the very easiest to the more complicated but all should be well within the reach of the average stitcher. I have included actual size templates as far as possible, but if necessary they can easily be enlarged, either on your printer or by using a photocopier. I do hope you'll enjoy making them and have as much fun as I did putting this collection together for you!

Helen xx

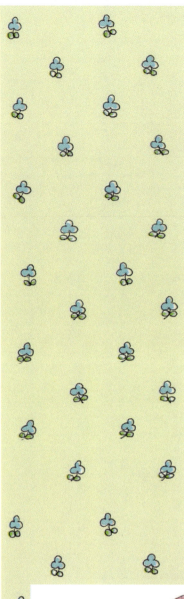

Getting Started

I love making softies - usually from scraps of felted knitwear, second hand tweeds and plaids, or even old blankets that might otherwise be discarded. Although the process itself isn't difficult (though it can sometimes be fiddly), too often the results are disappointing. This doesn't have to be the case - and I hope that you'll find my notes below useful - some of the tips were handed down to me - and others I've learned the hard way!

Choosing your materials:

Making softies needn't be an expensive craft. I make most of mine from scraps that would otherwise be thrown away. If you are watching costs though, don't try to economise using cheap materials. A recycled piece of good quality fabric will make a much nicer, longer-lasting softie than a flimsy, poor quality piece of fabric purchased especially for your project.

Look for old woollen or even - if you're very lucky! - cashmere knitwear in thrift or charity shops, or jumble sales - when felted these make wonderful softies - felted cashmere is particularly lovely for baby toys as it keeps its super-soft feel. Old blankets are also good and of course felt is the classic choice. Be sure to choose a good quality wool or wool-mix felt though as cheap acrylic craft felt is likely to tear at the seams and lose its colour in washing. I've also used medium-weight cotton or cotton-linen blend fabrics very successfully, though these are much less forgiving than woollen fabrics and felts as there is absolutely no "give" whatsoever so accurate cutting is essential.

Cotton prints should always be washed if you're using new fabric - this will remove any dressing and avoid possible future shrinkage of your softie.

Man made fibres are generally unsuitable for softie making. Shiny fabrics, such as silk, satin and heavily glazed cotton are also unsuitable. They fray too easily, pucker when sewn together and do not stuff or wash well.

Cutting your pattern pieces:

This is a very important part of the process. It's well worth taking a lot of time and care when cutting out as it'll pay dividends later on. Bad cutting will result in misshapen softies and pattern pieces that don't fit together properly.

Many people think that they should use small scissors to cut out fiddly pieces, such as the combs on the Two French Hens pattern - but this isn't necessarily the case. Felt pieces for these details must be cut out with a continuous action so giving a nice smooth line to the edge. A series of short cuts with small scissors may give you a jagged, unattractive-looking edge. I often use my large dressmaking shears to cut out these more detailed shapes!

Whatever scissors you're using, they must be nice and sharp. Don't be tempted to cut out the cardboard bases with your fabric shears as this will ruin their cutting edges.

If you're using a woven fabric, then make sure that the grain runs up and down the piece, not diagonally as this will cause it to stretch and distort.

Often it's nice to combine different fabrics in one softie, such as the little French Hen below who is created from vintage blanket, cotton fabrics and wool mix felt.

If you want to use cotton fabrics with exterior, decorative seams as I have in this little hen, then you will need to over-stitch the edges of your softie pieces before joining them together as otherwise they will fray. Use a machine zig-zag stitch in matching thread, or your overlocker/serger if you have one. You only need to do this if the fabric is part of the actual softie body - if you're using it for details such as the hen's wing, then it isn't necessary as the cut edge won't be under any strain.

Sewing your pieces together:

You can join your pieces either by hand or by machine stitching and each of these two methods will give your softie a completely different look. I much prefer to stitch by hand as there's more opportunity to tweak a little if necessary as I go - and I also like to stuff small pieces as I go rather than trying to push stuffing into them at the end. Stuffing as you go is almost impossible when machine sewing your softie.

My favourite way to join pieces by hand is to place wrong sides together, then stitch over the seams with half cross stitch in one direction, then returning the other way. I do it like this for two reasons. Firstly, it makes a lovely decorative effect and secondly for strength. If one thread gets broken chances are that its partner which will have been stitched coming back the other way will hold firm until you have chance to repair your softie.

The thread you choose for sewing the pieces together can either match your materials - the best choice for machine sewing - or contrast/complement them - great for hand stitching and making a feature of the seams.

If you're new to softie making you may like to tack (baste) your pieces together before you begin to stitch. It's not a good idea to use pins as they could accidentally be left in the toy. Also, as the softies are quite small, pins are a bit bulky and don't really work very well.

Stuffing your softie:

This is a very important step, and is well worth taking time and trouble over. The amount of stuffing you use and how you insert it will determine your softie's final shape.

If making a softie for a child then you should always use new stuffing that meets legal requirements for toys, particularly in respect of fire. If your softie is going to be for decorative purposes only, then you can economise by using chopped up old tights, old cushion filling, or even cotton wool if you're really stuck!

You must be happy with the shape and feel of your softie before you close the final seam as it's impossible to rearrange the stuffing once that seam is closed. The only way to alter anything at this point is to open the seam, take the stuffing out and start again!

If your softie has a flat base, like the pin cushion mice or hens, then you will need to insert a piece of cardboard into the base to ensure it remains flat when stuffed and your softe will stand nicely. You can also insert rice, polybeads or even (my favourite) a rounded beach pebble into the base to weight your softie and stop it wobbling over. Don't do this if it's intended for a young child though.

Always stuff the extremities first, using very small quantities of stuffing to begin with to avoid gaps and lumpiness. I like to stuff and sew the seams as I go for hard to reach places, but you can also use the blunt end of a knitting needle, pencil or even your stuffing stick (see below) to push the stuffing into place. It's much better to have an over rather than an under-stuffed softie. If it's too soft it will soon develop a wobbly head and floppy limbs if played with. Stuffing will always compact rather than expand.

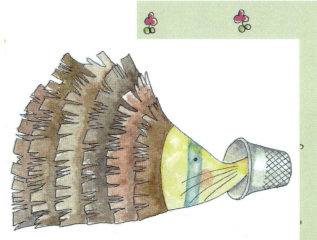

Stuffing Stick: This is the only specialised tool I use when softie making - though I think to call it a tool is quite a grand title for it! All you need is an ordinary bamboo skewer. Break off the pointed end and "fray" the bottom slightly. This will enable your stick to grab the stuffing while you're pushing it into those hard-to-reach places - so the stuffing won't compact and become lumpy.

Finishing details:

The positioning of details such as eyes and ears will give each softie an individual character and moving them only slightly will completely alter your softie's expression. Make sure that these parts are very firmly attached and if your softie is intended for a young child then don't use items that might cause choking such as buttons, ribbons and bells.

And finally:

Have confidence and don't give up part way through! Many softies don't look good until they're finally finished with all the little details so important to create their characters are finished. So stick with the project and I'm sure you'll be delighted with the results!

The softie patterns on the following pages were first published in the Bustle & Sew Magazine between 2011 and 2013. You can learn more about the magazine - a monthly stitching e-mag over on the Bustle & Sew website:

www.bustleandsew.com/magazine

The patterns in this book are graded 1, 2 or 3 star according to how easy they are to make - 1 star is the easiest, but all are within the reach of the average stitcher.

Pin Cushion Mice *

A Bustle & Sew classic, I originally released my take on this old-fashioned method of making these little mice back in March 2011.

They turned out to be one of my most popular free patterns ever - and now they're back - and looking even more cute for 2013. They're really easy to make - great for fetes, bazaars or for making with children - you'll have a dozen of the little creatures sitting in a row before you know it!

You will need:

- 9" square felt for body and ears
- 6" square contrast fabric for tail and ears
- 3" square cardboard to stiffen base
- Rice or poly beads to weight base (optional)
- Polyfil for stuffing body
- Stranded embroidery floss in suitable colour to sew body
- Black stranded embroidery floss for eyes and nose- or use small round black beads if preferred - but this means the mouse will not be suitable for a small child. .
- Dark brown strong thread for whiskers (optional)

To make your mouse:

- Cut out all pieces as shown on template
- Cut a strip of fabric for the tail 4" long x 1 ½" wide.
- Fold ¼" under along each long side, and then fold in half.
- Tuck one short edge in for the tip of the tail and secure with a few small stitches.
- Using 3 strands of embroidery floss, blanket stitch along the open side of the tail to secure. Set to one side.
- Stitch the bottom edge of the body to the circular base with wrong sides together. First work half-cross stitch in one direction, then return and over stitch in half-cross stitch in the other direction using 3 strands of floss. . Then stitch up the back for ½" in the same way, wrong sides together.
- Insert the unfinished end of the tail with the blanket stitched seam facing upwards and secure in place with small stitches.
- Continue up the back for a further 1". Leave a 1 ½" gap for stuffing and then stitch up to the nose.
- Insert the cardboard circle into the base to keep it flat.
- Stuff the nose end using small pieces of stuffing to avoid lumpiness.
- Pour rice or granules if using into the base and then add stuffing to body. When you are happy with the shape, close the back seam.
- Make the ears by placing the pairs of outers and inners together, wrong sides facing and cross stitch around the outer curved edge. Fold the base edge in half and secure with a few stitches, then flatten the seam and position ears on head, either side of the centre back seam so they will frame the mouse's face.
- The eyes are French knots worked with black floss - or stitch round black beads into place if using. The whiskers are strong thread - catch them in place with a small stitch under the nose so they can't be easily pulled out. Oversew the tip of the nose with black thread.
- FINISHED!

Template page 50

Two French Hens *

"Deux poules Francais"

Adorable little hen softies stitched from felt and fabric scraps. Each hen measures about 4 ½" high. They're a great beginners' project or a really quick and easy make for the more experienced stitcher. A French Hen would make a lovely door stop if she was a little larger – or why not part-stuff and add a lining for a cute egg cosy?

You will need:

- 2" square felt or similar for the body
- 4" square felt or similar for the head
- Scraps of red felt for comb and wattles
- 4" square fabric or felt for wings
- Small piece of cardboard for base
- Tiny black beads for eyes (eighth of an inch)
- Rice or poly beads to weight base (optional)
- Stranded cotton embroidery floss in suitable colour for body plus tiny bit of black thread for attaching eyes. You will use 3 strands of floss when joining the body pieces.
- Toy stuffing

To make your hen:

- Cut pieces as shown on template. Sew the head and body pieces together along the line a – c. Place wrong sides together and stitch by hand using half cross stitch one way, then working back the other way to complete the cross stitch over the seams. Join the front of the body from a – e.
- Attach the base to the body in the same way.
- Join the front of the head from c to just before d.
- Stitch the wattles to the seam with a couple of tiny pieces.
- Insert the beak at d and secure between the two sides using tiny stitches, then oversew with cross stitch. Do the same with the wattle and then close the head seam from d to a.
- Close the back seam from b to the top of the tail and insert your cardboard base.
- Add rice/poly beads to weight base if using.
- Stuff your hen, paying particular attention to her head, using small pieces of stuffing and moulding her head into shape.
- Close the top seam, adding more stuffing to shape the tail as you go.
- Sew wings into position using straight stitches. This is done at this stage to make sure you like their position.
- Mark the position of her eyes with pins - move them around until you're happy with her expression, then stitch in place with black thread.
- FINISHED!!

I added little hearts to this hen's wings to make her even cuter! Cut and attach them in exactly the same way as the wings.

Template Page 51

Bustle & Sew
Love to Sew and Sew with Love .....

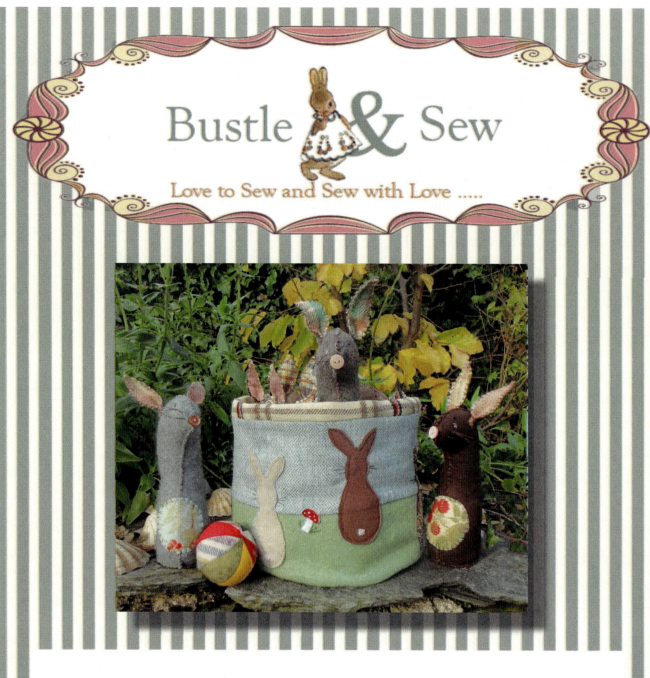

A Muddle of Bunnies *

Nine little bunnies, a tub to keep them in and a ball to knock them over with – so easy to sew .. and hours of fun for the family!!   Bunnies are weighted at the base and have little patchwork tummies - you could always add numbers or names to their patches!

Each bunny measures 10" tall to the tips of his ears.

You will need:

For the bunnies:

- 9 x 10" squares fabric for bodies – use a medium to heavy-weight fabric
- 9 x 3" squares fabric for tummies – a lighter weight quilting fabric is nice – choose prints that work well to contrast with the bodies
- 9 x 3" squares fabric for insides of ears – felt is nice – needs to be medium to heavy-weight so ears will stand up nicely
- 9 x small (no larger than ½") buttons for noses
- 9 x ½" pom poms for tails
- Pink and black embroidery floss
- Perle thread or cotton floss to stitch bunnies' seams - choose colours that work well with your fabrics.
- Strong dark brown thread
- 1 piece of A4 or Letter size medium weight card for bases
- 9 x smooth beach pebbles to weight bases (you can use polybeads or rice, but make sure they're contained within muslin bags in the body of each bunny as otherwise they might leak). PS. Don't use rice if you think you might want to wash your bunnies!!
- Toy stuffing
- Hot glue gun (optional)

For the ball:

- 8 x differently coloured fabric scraps in felt or other medium weight fabric each measuring 5"x 2"
- Smooth pebble to weight ball
- Toy stuffing

For the storage tub:

- 35" x 8" piece of canvas for lining
- 11" circle of canvas for base
- 10" circle of medium to heavy weight card for base
- 35" x 3 ½" piece of green fabric
- 11" circle of green fabric for base
- 35" x 4 ½" piece of blue or blue mix fabric
- 35" x 2 ½" piece of cream or cream mix fabric
- 7 x 6" x 3" pieces of felt or other fabric for bunnies' bodies.
- Tiny scraps of red and white felt for toadstools.
- Cream, green and black stranded cotton floss.
- Bondaweb or fabric adhesive as preferred.

¼" seam allowances throughout unless otherwise stated

To make bunnies:

- Cut one body piece on fold of main fabric as indicated for each bunny.
- Cut two ears and one base in main fabric
- Cut 2 ears in contrast fabric
- Cut 1 tummy in printed fabric
- With 3 strands of cotton floss or Perle cotton and wrong sides of bunny together stitch bunny seam from A to B and C to D. As these bunnies are going to get a lot of wear, I recommend using half cross stitch working first in one direction in half- cross stitch, then returning the other way. Then if a thread breaks, the second should hold the bunny together until you can repair him. Stitch base to main body
- Stuff bunny firmly to point B, then insert cardboard base (use the circle on the template, but cut it a little smaller to fit comfortably into base.

- Wrap pebble in stuffing and place on top of cardboard base, then finish stuffing bunny and close seam from B to C.
- Stitch fronts and backs of ears together with half cross stitch, fold in half vertically at base, securing with a few stitches.
- Position ears on sides of head, and when you're happy with their positioning, stitch them firmly into place.
- Position tummy and secure with straight stitches (see photos for guide on positioning)
- Stitch eyes with black, and cheeks with pink floss (make sure they're level on either side of the bunny's head!). Secure button to tip of nose.
- Add the whiskers using strong brown thread. Go in on one side near the nose, angling your stitch towards the bunny's nose, then take a tiny back stitch beneath the button before coming out on the other side of the nose. Leave a long loop then return and take another tiny back stitch beneath the button as before. Continue until you have enough whiskers, then snip loops and cut to the same length. Taking the tiny back stitches stops the whiskers from slipping out.
- Your bunny is now finished!

Make storage tub:

- Join your green, blue and cream strip of fabric along the long edges. Press seams flat. This makes the tub exterior.
- Trace the bunny shapes onto the paper side of your Bondaweb, then fuse to the reverse of the fabric you're using for these bunnies and cut out. Peel off paper backing and position bunnies as shown below (not to scale)
- When you're happy with the positioning of your bunny shapes, then fuse into place by ironing.
- Machine applique around the edges of your bunny using dark thread in your needle and a lighter colour in the bobbin to prevent the line of stitching looking too hard and solid. Go around each bunny twice.
- Stitch tails with cream floss and French knots - or if preferred you could use a small circle of white felt.
- Add the whiskers and scatter a few little felt toadstools - the stems are just tiny rectangles of white felt, and the tops semi-circles or elongated semi-circles. Work some grass around the toadstools in green floss.

- When your applique is finished press lightly on the reverse then, with wrong sides together join the two short sides by machine.

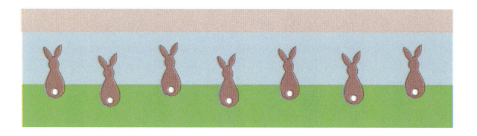

- With right sides together insert the 11" circle of green fabric as your base. Clip around the edges (but watch you don't snip your stitches!)

- Turn ¼" cream fabric (at the top of your tub) to inside and press firmly. Then turn ¾" over and press again.

- Make the lining by joining the two short edges of your inner fabric and inserting the 11" circle as the base, snipping the circular seam as before.

- Insert card circle into base of outer, then insert lining into outer, wrong sides together.

- Tuck the top edge under the turned over part of cream fabric, then slip stitch into place.

- FINISHED!!

To make the ball:

- Join your fabric segments together – do this in 2 sets of four, then join the sets leaving a gap down one side for stuffing.

- Turn right side out and check all your seams carefully. If the points don't quite match at the top, just cut 2 small circles of felt and when your ball is finished, stitch these to the ball at top and bottom to cover the joins.

- Wrap pebble in stuffing, partly stuff ball and then insert pebble. Continue stuffing until ball is round and firm, then stitch gap closed.

- FINISHED!!

Template Page 52

Flying Pig Softies *

These little pigs look far too solid to be real flying pigs.…. more as though they have rummaged around in their dressing-up box and found some wings to attach to their plump little bodies.

They are really easy to make – most of the sewing is done by hand, apart from the wings which I have sewn by machine, though you could hand stitch these if you wanted.

You will need:

- 12" square of felt or felted wool in your chosen colour for the pig's body.

- 6" square of light weight cotton fabric for his wings

- Small pink button for nose

- Two small black beads for eyes

- 12" x 1 ½" rectangle of cotton fabric for pig's middle

- Stranded cotton floss in pink (and another colour if you prefer to stitch his seams)

- Tiny piece of pink ric-rac braid

- Toy stuffing

To make your pig:

Note: the templates are given at full size

- Cut out all pieces using the template at the end of the pattern. Cut the body pieces from your felt and 2 wing shapes from your light-weight fabric.

- Using either blanket stitch or cross stitch - whichever you prefer - stitch the underbelly pieces to the main body pieces from A to B around legs and trotters.

- Now attach the top gusset on one side. Start at point A and carefully easy the gusset around your pig's snout. The narrowest part of the gusset should join the very tip of his snout. Then continue stitching up his back and around to his bottom. Don't worry if your fabric stretches a little and you don't quite make point B - it's not a disaster and he'll look fine - just with a slightly squarer rear end. If you overshoot, then trim the excess to a point and match point B (this pattern is very forgiving).

- Attach the second main body to the top gusset in the same way. It is VERY IMPORTANT that you match the gusset at point A, otherwise your pig will have a wonky snout! Keep checking that all seems fine while you're stitching around his snout.

- Close the gap between his underbelly pieces for 1 ½" back and front, leaving a gap in the centre for stuffing.

- Stuff your pig's body quite firmly, pushing the stuffing well down into his legs and snout, moulding and squeezing as you go to achieve the best shape. Only insert small pieces at a time to avoid lumpiness.

- Close your stuffing gap. If his legs splay out to widely, then fold them in towards his belly and stitch a dart to keep them beneath his body.

- Fold the ears in half vertically and secure them at the base with a few stitches.

- Position on the sides of your pig's head and stitch into place.

- Use glass-headed pins to trial the position of your pig's eyes - this is very important as the positioning of his eyes will affect his final expression. When you're happy with their positions sew on the two little black beads. Pull your stitches quite firmly to add contour to his face. If you're making the pig for a child you might prefer to use safety eyes or embroider the pig's eyes instead.

- Take your long rectangle of cotton fabric and press under ¼" on both sides.

- Wrap the rectangle around the pig's body pulling snugly and turning under the raw edges of one end which will overlap the other. (you may need to shorten your rectangle - I have deliberately given you a generous length to fit even the fattest pig!)

- With the overlap at the bottom of the pig on his belly seam, secure the fabric band to the pig with a few small stitches - at that point only - there's no need to go all around the band.

- Stitch cheeks with a few small straight stitches using your pink floss. Attach button for nose (omit if making for a child).

- Stitch your wings to the top of the pig making sure the stitches go through both the band and the felt of the pig's body.

- Place your wing pieces right sides together and machine stitch around the edges, leaving a gap for turning and stuffing as shown on the diagram.

- Finally the tail - attach the tiny piece of pink ric-rac braid to your pig's rear, curl it around and secure with a few stitches.

- Turn right side out and stuff lightly. Top stitch the stuffing gap closed.

- FINISHED!!

- Machine or hand stitch along the red dotted lines on the diagram to represent the contours of the wings

Template Page 54

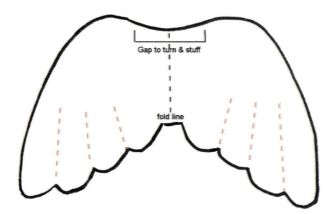

- With top sides together, fold your wings in half along the dotted line on the diagram and machine stitch from front to back of wings ¼" from the fold. This will give your pig's wings a nice feeling of "lift".

Hodge and Podge the Hedgehog Softies **

Who could resist these adorable little hedgehog softies?

There's Podge - the little baby hedgehog, and Hodge, her big brother dressed in a smart stripey scarf to keep out those autumn chills (seen here with his cousins Horace and Humphrey).

You will need for Podge:

- 8" square old blanket/felt for body
- 2 yards x 1" wide strips of tweedy/woollen fabric for prickles
- 2 small black beads for eyes
- ¼" button for nose
- Strong dark brown thread for whiskers
- Small round pebble
- Small piece of cardboard
- Brown thread for your sewing machine
- Toy stuffing

Note: If making for a young child, then embroider the features with cotton embroidery floss and omit the pebble in the base.

¼" seam allowance is included in template

Method:

- Cut out your felt/fabric - cut 2 body pieces (reversing one if your fabric has a right and wrong side)
- Cut 1 base piece in felt/fabric, then cut another piece in cardboard approx ¼" smaller all the way around
- Take your strips of tweedy fabric and cut into them at about ¼" intervals to make a fringe. Be careful only to cut in about ¾ " - don't cut all the way through!
- Position the strips vertically on each Podge's body shapes starting from the back and working towards her head. Machine stitch to the body and cut the strips to length as you go along. Make sure the spines (fringe) are towards the back of the body and that you have a good overlap so she doesn't have any bare spots!)
- When attaching your last few strips, make sure they're slightly curved (line E to F on the template shows where the last strip is placed).

- Now sew the two body pieces together around the back and head from X to Y with right sides facing. Some of your prickles will be included in the seam, but that's fine, you can probably tease out a few with a blunt needle afterwards, and the seam isn't very noticeable among all the fringe ends.
- Turn Podge right side out and stuff. Work very small pieces of stuffing into the end of her nose and face, shaping her with your hands as you go.
- Stuff the body firmly, then insert your pebble towards the base.
- Place cardboard base on top of pebble so she will stand firmly.
- Finally place felt/fabric base on the cardboard and top stitch all the way around the body opening to close the body completely - you will need to do this by hand.

- Using strong thread attach black beads for eyes and button for nose.

- Stitch whiskers with strong thread - leaving loops at each side of the snout and taking a small back stitch beneath the nose to secure whiskers in place.

You will need for Hodge:

- 12" square old blanket/felt for body
- 4 yards x 1" wide strips of tweedy/woollen fabric for prickles
- 2 small black beads for eyes
- 2" button for nose
- Strong dark brown thread for whiskers
- Small round pebble
- Small piece of cardboard
- Brown thread for your sewing machine
- 4 ply yarn for scarf (if knitting or crocheting)
- Toy stuffing

Note: If making for a young child, then embroider the features with cotton embroidery floss and omit the pebble in the base.

¼" seam allowance is included in template

To make Hodge:

- Cut out all pieces from the template. Cut 1 base piece in felt or your body fabric, then cut another in cardboard about ¼" smaller all the way round to fit inside your base when sewing up your toy.

- With right sides facing sew together back pieces from A to B. Turn right side out and press.

- Take your strips of tweedy fabric and cut points along one edge to form spines (see template for diagram).

- Position the strips horizontally on Hodge's back (see dotted lines on template for your guide) starting from the bottom and working upwards towards his head.

- Machine stitch to the body and cut the strips to length as you go along. Make sure the spines (points) are downwards towards the base of the body and that you have a good overlap so he doesn't have any bare spots!) If you do have any bare patches then simply stitch in another row of spines - hedgehogs are not very neat animals. If you find it too tricky to use your machine as you get towards the shaping at the top of the back, then simply attach the strips by hand with a firm back stitch.

- Place your two front body pieces together with right sides facing and join from A to D.

- Sew each pair of arms together with right sides facing, leaving the short edges open. Clip curves and turn right side out. Stuff lightly and tack to body front positioning as shown on the template.

- Repeat for the legs.

- Sew the front and back of the body together from A to D with right sides facing. Turn right side out and remove tacking stitches.

- Stuff body firmly inserting your pebble at the base, then finishing with a little more stuffing and your cardboard base. Join your felt base to the body with cross stitch.

- Secure eyes and nose to body and make whiskers with strong thread as before.

- I knitted Hodge's scarf with 4-ply yarn and 2 ¾ mm needles (US fingering or sport and US needles size 2) in garter stitch - 7 stitches to each row. You could crochet his scarf or simply use a strip of fabric frayed at the ends if you don't knit or crochet.

Template Page 55

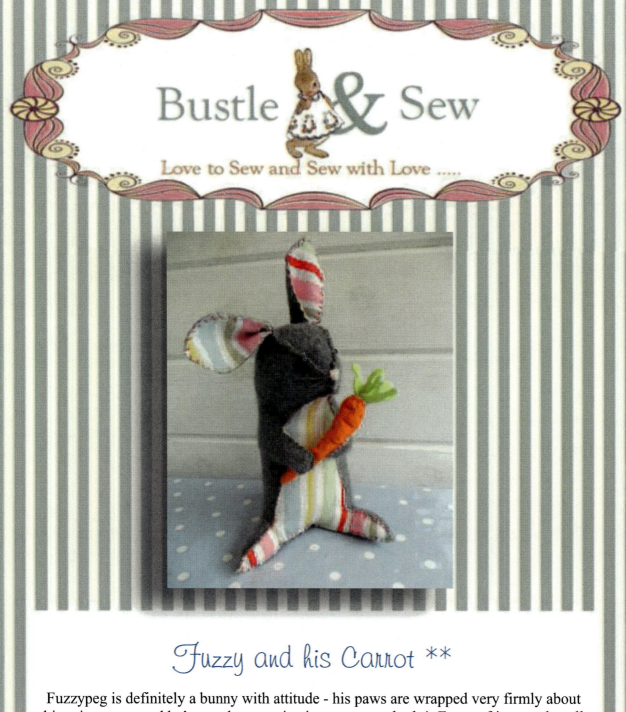

Fuzzy and his Carrot **

Fuzzypeg is definitely a bunny with attitude - his paws are wrapped very firmly about his prize carrot and he's not about to give it away to anybody! Easy softie to make, all hand sewn.

Fuzzypeg measures 12" tall from his fuzzy tail to the tips of his ears.

You will need:
- 16" x 12" piece of grey felt for main body and ears
- 10" square piece of stripey fabric for tummy and ear linings
- 7" x 5" piece of orange felt for carrot
- 2" x 6" piece of green felt for carrot leaves
- Tiny scrap of light pink felt for nose
- 2 x 8 mm (¼") safety eyes
- Stranded cotton floss in light pink, orange, dark orange and variegated colours
- White woollen yarn to make pompom for tail
- Two cardboard rings or pompom maker
- Toy stuffing
- Temporary fabric marker pen

Making your Fuzzypeg:

Fuzzypeg is hand-stitched and his seams are joined with cross stitch. You do this by placing the wrong sides together and joining one way using half cross stitch, then return in the opposite direction to finish your stitch. This gives your seams extra strength since, if one thread is broken the whole seam won't unravel. It's also a nice decorative finish. Use 2 strands of variegated floss.

- Cut out all pieces according to instructions on the templates. The templates are given at 80% of actual size - but size really doesn't matter - if you don't enlarge them your Fuzzypeg will simply be a little smaller than mine.
- Start by joining the two main body pieces from the centre of the back down to X marked on the template.
- Join the inner body along the bottom edge working from X outwards to the end of each paw and back again.
- Join the muzzle from B to C on the template and then finish joining the inner body. You will need to ease the outer fabric around the inner - it does go - I promise, and easing it round in this way gives Fuzzypeg nice plump limbs.
- Place the outer and inner ear pieces right sides together and stitch around edges in the same way.
- Insert head gusset matching at C. Fold each ear in half vertically and insert at E as you stitch.
- Stitch 1" down from the end of the head gusset.
- Lightly stuff your head and determine the position of the eyes. I usually use black glass-headed pins for this and then mark the spot with my temporary fabric marker pen. Do take care over this stage as the positioning of the eyes will affect your Fuzzypeg's final expression. When you're totally happy with the positioning of the eyes, mark the spot, remove the stuffing and insert the safety eyes.
- Stuff Fuzzypeg. Use a stuffing stick (bamboo skewer with the pointy end broken off and the end frayed to "grab" the stuffing) to push small pieces of stuffing into his limbs and muzzle. You can mould his body with your hands as you stuff - I chose to mould him slightly to the left and upwards
- Make sure you stuff him firmly as stuffing will compress over time and you don't want him to become limp and floppy. Stitch the gap closed.

Template Page 57

Swan Softie Pattern ***

These little swans measure 9" tall and are a great way to use vintage blanket or felt pieces. They are not intended to be given to children as toys.

They're probably not a beginner's project, but if you have some experience of softie making then you'll discover that they take more time and patience than skill. There is some simple wiring - just a single piece to support the neck.

You will need:

- 14" x 20" piece of felt, woollen fabric or old blanket (must be non-stretchy and not easy to fray)
- 8" x 10" contrast fabric for insides of wings
- 10" x 3" felt for base (or alternatively cut from your large piece of felt, there will be enough)
- Scraps of orange and black felt
- 12" garden wire
- 2 x 1" buttons for base of wings
- 2 x ⅛ " shiny black beads for eyes
- Black and orange cotton floss
- Floss to harmonise with the colours of your fabric (for stitching seams)
- Round pebble (about 2" long)
- Medium weight card
- Good quality toy stuffing
- Stuffing stick *
- Curved needle & long (eg sashiko needle)

Method:

- Cut out your pieces from the template on the following pages. To fit the page size he template is given slightly smaller than the size swan I made, but I have included the exact measurements of two of the pieces to enable you to resize if you wish. Of course you can make a smaller (or indeed larger!) swan if you wish.

- The pieces are joined by placing right sides together and working over the edges with cross stitch in 2 strands of floss. Work half-cross stitches in one direction first, then return and complete the stitch in the other direction. This gives your seam added strength as if the thread breaks in one place, it won't completely unravel.

- First join the head gusset to the body pieces, working from A to B on both sides.

- Now join the top seam from B to C and then the under-body piece on both sides from C to D, leaving a gap for stuffing as shown.

- Join beneath beak from X to Z

- Take your piece of wire and bend it into a loop at both ends. You can bind with tape if preferred but I didn't do this.

- Bend your wire to the shape of the neck as shown by the dotted line on the template

- Stuff the top of the head and add stuffing to the back of the neck, then insert the wire so that it extends into the body and head as shown on the template.

- Stuff your head firmly around the wire (use your stuffing stick*) with small pieces of stuffing - if you add large pieces your head will become lumpy.

- Continue stuffing down into the neck, making sure the wire is firmly embedded in the stuffing and that you have no lumps. Sew from X to Y as you stuff. Use half cross stitch as before, returning to complete the stitch when the neck is finished.

- Part stuff body, then insert pebble to give swan stability. Surround pebble with stuffing and then insert your card base to give your swan a nice flat firm bottom to stand on.

- To make the beak, join the two upper pieces on the wrong side from G to F using cross stitch as before.

- Put the black and orange pieces of the under-beak together and stitch all round with running stitch and 2 strands of orange floss.

- Now join upper beak to under beak, with running stitch, matching the letters shown on the template.

- Note: the orange part of the lower beak is on the outside and black on the inside. This makes a clear dividing line where the beak would open in a real swan and adds a lot of character.

- Stuff the beak firmly and sew to the head with small stitches. You will probably find it easiest to use a curved needle for this. Note the positioning and angle of the beak as shown in the photo on the right.

- Take a couple of small stitches at the top of the black part of the beak just above the fold - to make a little tuck in the black felt.

- Attach to head with black floss and curved needle using the photo below as a guide.

- Make up the wings as for the body, then stuff very lightly. Indicate feathers by stitching running stitch lines as shown on the template.

- Attach wings to body as shown in the photo on the left, aligning the bottoms of the wings with the base seam of the body.

- Add your two 1" buttons at the base of the wings as shown. Using your long needle stitch right through the body and pull the buttons tightly against the body - moulding the body shape inwards to make the wings firm and the body nicely rounded.

- Finally attach the two small black beads for eyes. Again pull them firmly against the head so that they sit in two little indentations, giving shape and character to your swan.

FINISHED!!

* Don't forget - a stuffing stick is really handy to push your stuffing up into those hard-to-reach areas. Simply snap the point off a bamboo skewer and "fray" the end slightly so it will grab the stuffing as you push. Easy - but so useful!

Template Page 59

Mounted Deer Head ✱✱✱

No deer were harmed in the making of this softie! Here's a cruelty free deer head mounted on a 6" hoop that measures 14" from the bottom of his neck to the tips of his antlers.

Wiring in his antlers make them nice and firm and card at the back of the hoop stops the head flopping forward.

You will need:

12" square woollen/felt fabric for head

18" x 9" quilting weight cotton fabric for antlers

9" square canvas or heavy interfacing for antlers

2 x 13mm safety eyes

Small scrap of pink fabric/felt for inners of ears

2" square scrap fabric for nose

8" square medium weight fabric for hoop

8" square card to back hoop

Brown and blue stranded cotton embroidery floss

2 x ¼" buttons for nostrils.

Toy stuffing

22" length galvanised garden wire

Temporary fabric spray adhesive

Temporary fabric marker pen

Hot glue gun (you can use PVA glue but allow for drying time)

6" wooden embroidery hoop

To make the antlers:

- Cut your cotton fabric into two 9" squares. Make a sandwich with the interfacing/canvas as follows: Cotton fabric right side down, interfacing/canvas, cotton fabric right side up.

- Lightly spray the layers with temporary fabric adhesive to hold them together.
- Take your antler template and place it on the top layer.
- Draw around it with your temporary fabric marker pen, then flip it over and draw around it again.

- Machine stitch all along the lines you have drawn, leaving the ends open.
- Now cut out your antlers. Cut ¼" outside the lines you drew and stitched over. Use large shears and make long smooth cuts, moving the fabric rather than the shears.
- Machine zig-zag around the edges of the antlers. Remove your lines.

- Take your galvanised wire and bend over 1" at each end to form a loop.
- Bend the wire into a "U" shape and then bend again to form the antler shape (indicated by the dotted lines on the template).

- Push the wire up into the antler shapes between the cotton and interfacing.

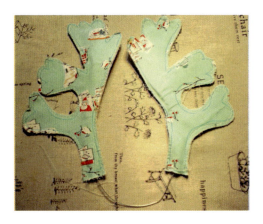

- Pin into place through all layers of fabric/interfacing and the wire loops

Assemble the Head:

- Cut out the two head pieces, one gusset and four ear pieces.

- Place a felt and pink fabric ear piece wrong sides together and stitch around three edges using cross stitch (work half in one direction, then turn around and come back the other way). Don't stitch the bottom of the ear as this will be hidden within the head.

- Place the ears to one side for the moment.

- Using the template as a guide, mark the positions of the eyes with your pen.

- Stitch the two sides of the neck in the same way together with wrong sides together from A to C.

- Now insert the gusset. Stitch up both sides of the head from A to the first X marking the position of the antlers.

- Stuff the nose part of the head

- Place the antlers so that the bottom of the "U" shape is inside the head and then add more stuffing around the U.

- This is a bit fiddly, but now you need to stitch the antlers into place within the seams. Do each side in turn, holding firmly in place, . Don't worry if they flop forwards, you can easily re-position them and when you complete stuffing the head they will remain in place.

- Continue along each side seam to the X marking the position of the ears.

- Fold your ear shape in half vertically with the pink side innermost, then stitch into the seam.

- Insert the safety eyes before completing the stitching.

- Complete stitching to the back of the neck.

- Now, holding the antlers in their correct position, stuff the head very firmly, moulding the stuffing all around the "U" shape at the bottom of the wire.

- Close the back seam from B to C adding more stuffing if needed as you go. The head must be stuffed firmly or the antlers will flop forward and it won't sit properly on the hoop.

- Cut a nose shape from your brown fabric and stitch into place on the head. Embroider the mouth and add two small buttons for the nostrils.

- The head is now finished.

Assemble the mounted head:

- Place your medium weight fabric in the hoop, if it's directional then make sure it's straight and the right way up (the screw will be at the top of the hoop).

- Screw as tightly as you can. Trim fabric to within ½" of edge of hoop, press under and hold in place with glue.

- Cut a circle of card to fit the inside of the hoop and glue in place.

- Now take your reindeer head and run a line of glue right the way down the back seam and spread it either side so that it covers about ½" strip at the back of the neck.

- Press neck very firmly against the fabric in the hoop and hold into place until the glue has set.

- The head is very light and this should be all that is necessary to sit it firmly upon the mount.

- If your head does flop forward, then you can push a sharp bamboo skewer through from the back of the hoop and up into the neck and then glue the other end into place at the back of the hoop, but this shouldn't really be necessary.

FINISHED!!

Template Page 61

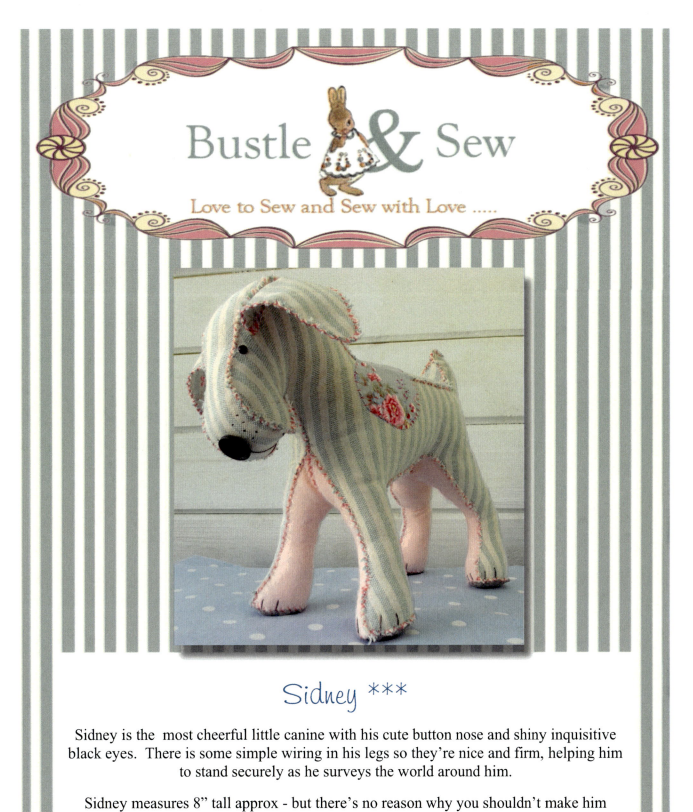

Sidney ***

Sidney is the most cheerful little canine with his cute button nose and shiny inquisitive black eyes. There is some simple wiring in his legs so they're nice and firm, helping him to stand securely as he surveys the world around him.

Sidney measures 8" tall approx - but there's no reason why you shouldn't make him larger or smaller - just resize the pattern accordingly.

You will need:

- ½ yard stripey fabric (you may be able to manage with less if you are using a non-directional fabric)
- 12" square pink felt
- 4" square grey felt
- 5 mm (¼" black safety eyes)
- ¾" black or dark brown button
- Pink and dark brown stranded cotton floss
- 8" square floral printed fabric
- 1 yard (just under 1 m) galvanised wire
- Fabric adhesive tape (a roll of sticking plaster is good for this - don't use expensive tape)
- Toy stuffing

Cut pieces: *(seam allowances are included)*

- 2 body shapes and 2 ears in main fabric (if your fabric has a right and wrong side don't forget to reverse your templates)
- 2 underbody gussets in pink felt
- 4 paw pads in grey felt
- 1 top body gusset in main fabric
- 2 ears and some nice rounded patches in floral print fabric

Notes:

- I always draw around my templates on the right side of the fabric with a temporary fabric marker. Then I can easily erase any lines that remain once my softie is finished.
- Half-cross stitch is a great stitch to use for making nice strong softie seams. Place your fabric wrong sides together. Work half-cross stitch in one direction using two strands of cotton floss, then return the other way. This means that if one thread is broken, the other isn't "related" to it and so will most probably hold until you can make a repair.
- The fabric I used was quite loosely woven so as I like to make my softies with the seams on the outside, after cutting the pieces I secured the edges with a machine zig-zag stitch to prevent fraying. I used matching thread and simply joined the seams over the top of the zig-zags which were then hardly noticeable.

Make up Sidney:

- With two strands of pink cotton floss join each underbody gusset to the body from B to C around the legs, eaving a 1 ½ - 2" gap at the front of each leg above the paw - this is to make it easier to insert and stuff around the wires.
- Insert paw pads
- Join underbody gusset along central seam, leaving a 3" gap for stuffing.
- Join top body gusset along one side from A to H.
- Join to second side from A to the back of the neck.
- Stuff head lightly and mark position of eyes

- Complete stitching the top gusset.
- Bend the wire over in half so that the legs are 2" apart and turn 2" forwards into a loop shape for each foot.
- Bend the hind legs to follow the shape of the pattern.
- Bind all rough edges with the adhesive tape so they don't poke through the softie fabric.
- Start with the front legs - place a small amount of stuffing in the bottom of each leg then insert the wire. Holding it carefully in place stuff all around it, inserting small pieces of stuffing through the gap you left in the front of the leg. Make sure the leg wires are well covered then stitch up the front gap. Push more stuffing down into the leg so that it's stuffed very firmly.
- Repeat with the other leg and then the back legs.
- Stuff the rest of the toy very firmly and close the bottom gusset.
- Join ear pieces wrong side together and attach to the side of the head.

- With 2 strands of brown floss attach button to nose and scatter a few tiny straight stitches to represent whiskers.

Wire insert for legs showing how to bind the rough edges.

Template Page 64

- Stitch claws onto feet with straight stitches, burying the end of your floss inside the softie.
- Add patches, securing to body with short straight stitches in pink floss.
- Bend legs into correct position and stand.
- FINISHED!!

Brave Aviator Mouse **

"Chocks Away! Ready for take off!"

This daring mouse aviator is ready to take to the air in his old-fashioned plane with button wheels.

Finished plane measures 8" long and 11 ½" from wing-tip to wing-tip.

You will need:

- 18" square of felt, or equivalent in scraps of woollen fabric for plane
- 2" x 4" cream felt for propeller
- 2" square lightweight card for propellor
- Tiny scraps of brown felt/blanket for mouse
- Even tinier scrap of black felt for helmet
- 12" length of garden wire
- Self-adhesive fabric tape
- Black embroidery floss for mouse features
- Strong thread for whiskers
- 36" twine for plane trim
- Lightweight yarn for scarf, or you could use a strip of fabric and fray the ends
- 2 large buttons for wheels and smaller button for centre of propeller
- Hot glue gun (or you could use PVA glue but will need to allow for drying time)
- Curved needle (optional but will make stitching plane together much easier)
- Polyester stuffing

NOTE: Seam allowance is ¼"

Method:

- Cut out pieces from the template. The plane body should measure 8 ½" long - you may need to resize depending upon your printer settings. You should cut:
- 4 wing pieces
- 2 tail fins
- 2 side bodies of plane
- 2 mouse pieces
- 2 mouse helmets
- 2 mouse ears
- 2 propellers

Make Plane:

- Place the two side bodies right sides together and machine stitch around the edges, leaving a 2" gap at the bottom for turning.

- Turn right side out and stuff firmly. Top stitch the gap closed.

- Sew the wing pieces together in pairs, right sides together, leaving the straight base edges open.

- Turn right side out and stuff firmly then, with your curved needle, sew to the body so that the front seam of each wing is about 1 ½" away from the plane nose. You may need to add a little more stuffing before you finally close the seam to make your wing nice and firm. If you don't have a curved needle then you can use a short straight needle, but your stitches will be larger and you may have to go around twice to fill in the gaps between them.

- Sew and stuff the tail fins in the same way and stitch them onto the main body so that the back seam is ¾" away from the centre seam at the back of the tail.

Make mouse aviator:

- With right sides together join your two mouse head pieces. Clip seam at tip of nose and clip curves. Turn right side out and stuff firmly

- Join two helmet pieces along long curved edge.

- Add a little stuffing to the top of the helmet

- Position helmet on mouse head and hand stitch into place with your black floss.

- Fold ears into a circular shape and stitch onto helmet

- Add features in black floss and whiskers in strong thread. When adding your whiskers don't just go from side to side, insert your needle towards the nose and make a tiny back stitch just beneath the nose before re-inserting your needle and bringing it out on the other side of the snout. This makes your whiskers nice and firm.

- Hand stitch your mouse to the top of the plane using the photo as a guide for positioning.

Make legs and propellor:

- Fold your garden wire in half, then into a "U" shape - each leg should be 2" long.

- Wrap the "U" shape with self-adhesive fabric tape.

- Cut 2 felt shapes for the propellor and one from card.

- Trim the card propellor shape so that it sits within the 2 felt shapes.

- Make a sort of sandwich of felt-card-felt and machine zig-zag around the edges. Now your propellor will be nice and firm.

Assemble plane:

- With your hot glue gun stick two buttons onto the end of the "U" shaped wire to represent wheels.

- Stick the top of the "U" to the underside of the plane approx 2 ½ " from the nose (use photo as guide).

- Glue propellor to front of nose, then glue button onto the centre of the propellor.

- Glue twine around wings/fins/mouse body to cover seams

- Finally knit your little mouse a scarf - I used 4 ply yarn (I think that's US fingering) and garter stitch, but just choose what suits you. Garter stitch is good though as it doesn't have a tendency to curl in at the edges. If you're not a knitter, then just cut a scrap of lightweight fabric instead and knot around you mouse's neck.

FINISHED!!

Template Pagae 66

Little Giraffe Softie **

Here's the sweetest little baby giraffe. He's a really simple shape, made special by stitching some basic felt squares to represent his patterning - and two little cheeks stitched with pink floss.

Measures approximately 11" tall.

You will need:

- 12" x 18" piece of light yellow felt or felted woollen jumper
- 9" square brown felt
- Dark brown wool
- Stranded cotton floss to match both colours of felt as well as pink and black.
- 2 x tiny black spherical beads for eyes
- ¼" button for nose
- Toy stuffing

Method:

All seams are joined on the outside. To do this place your pieces wrong sides together and work half-cross stitch in one direction, then back again in the other direction to form the whole stitch. This will give you nice strong, as well as decorative, seams.

- Cut 2 main body pieces, 1 head gusset and 2 body gusset pieces from light yellow felt
- Cut 4 feet from yellow felt
- Cut 8 hoof rectangles (as shown on template) and 8 feet from brown felt
- Cut 2 ears from brown felt
- Cut muzzle shapes as indicated on template from brown felt
- Cut two 1 ½" x 1" rectangles for horns from brown felt.
- Join body gussets around legs using matching floss. Insert feet pieces as you go.
- Join body pieces from B to X and insert head gusset from X to A. You may like to stuff as you go when joining second seam of head gusset to ensure neck is nice and firm and not lumpy.
- Stuff legs
- Join belly gussets from A to E and F to B, leaving gap for stuffing. Finish stuffing giraffe and close gap.
- Stitch muzzle pieces into place on muzzle.
- Make up hooves and stitch to bottom of legs.

- Cut squares and rectangles from brown felt - varying in size, but no larger than 1 ¼" x ¾" maximum and scatter over giraffe body, securing in place with small straight stitches.

- Roll up horn rectangles and stitch into place on head. Stitch ears, add beads for eyes (be sure to check positioning with pins first) and button for nose.

- Stitch mane into place down back of neck from between his horns to the end of the head gusset. Do this with your brown yarn, making loopy stitches with a back stitch in between each one to make sure the loops hold firmly. When you've completed the whole main snip and trim the loops, then brush them with a wire brush - or simply fluff with the end of your needle to tease apart the strands and make his mane very fluffy.

- For his tail, take three strands of wool, each measuring 8" through the giraffe at the end of the head gusset, leaving 4" free on either side.

- Divide into three groups of two, and plait together for about an inch. Knot the end, then trim the yarn and fluff as before.

Template Page 67

Felt Fox Head **

No foxes were harmed in the making of this trophy head - honestly! Mounted on an 8" hoop, this cheerful-looking little fox head measures around 9" tall with lovely floppy whiskers created from strong thread (easy!) and a cute black button nose.

Every home should have one!

- Place white ear interiors on top of fox red outers and stitch into place using small straight stitches at right angles to the edge of the white felt and then position and attach the pale pink pieces in the same way.

You will need:

- 18" square fox red felt
- 9" square white felt
- 3" square pale pink felt
- 2 x ¼" safety eyes
- 1" black button (for nose)
- Pale pink and fox red stranded cotton floss
- Strong brown thread
- Toy stuffing
- Hot glue gun
- 10" square cotton (non-stretchy) fabric for mounting
- 8" embroidery hoop

- Attach the chin pieces with white floss. Then turn over and trim away ⅛" from the edge of the fox red felt where it is overlapped by the white chin piece. This will stop it from peeking through when you join the chin seam (see below)

Method:

All seams are stitched with wrong sides together and half cross stitch worked first in one direction, then back again in the other direction

Use two strands of floss throughout.

- Cut all pieces as directed on templates.

- Join chin seam and insert head gusset matching point at X.

- Stuff head and determine position of eyes - test the position with glass-headed pins before you insert safety eyes as they can't be moved once fixed.

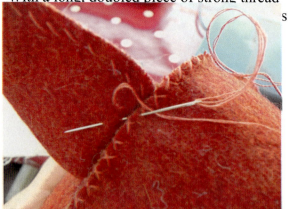

- When you're happy with the positioning of the eyes remove the stuffing and insert safety eyes. Then re-insert stuffing and stuff fox head, finally closing the seam at the back of the neck. Stuff firmly as you don't want him to flop forward when mounted.

- Gather bottoms of ears and then stitch into place at the sides of the head.

- Catch the sides of the ears to the seams of the head gusset, this will help them stay nice and upright.

- Stitch button into place on end of nose.

- With a long, doubled piece of strong thread

- Take tiny back stitches under the button to secure whiskers between loops, and then sprinkle a few tiny stitches on white part of muzzle. Add mouth in strong thread (see photo for guide)

Mount your fox head:

- Insert fabric into hoop and trim so there is 1" excess all around the hoop.

- Fold excess to back of hoop and glue to interior of hoop ring with your hot glue gun

- Spread hot glue on the back of the fox's neck, then press him firmly down onto the fabric in the hoop and hold there whilst glue dries (this doesn't take very long!)

- Your fox is now finished. If the head does droop (though if you've stuffed and glued firmly then it shouldn't, you can always poke a bamboo skewer through from the back of the hoop to help hold him firmly).

Template Page 70

Bustle and Sew Magazine

Before we get to the templates I just wanted to tell you a little bit about my [Bustle & Sew Magazine](#) - positively the nicest and best way to build your collection of Bustle & Sew patterns - and where all the patterns in this collection first appeared.

The Bustle & Sew magazine is a monthly e-magazine delivered direct to your email in-box on the last Thursday of each month ready to read as a pdf file – which is quick and easy to download and print.

So if you're like me and have a stash of irresistible fabrics, just waiting for you to find the perfect project to show them off in all their glory, I'm sure you'll enjoy my magazine.

Why not try it and see what you think? And there's no risk to you … if for any reason, or no reason at all, you decide not to continue with your subscription, then all you need to do is drop me an email to cancel. That's it - no penalties and no tie-in period.

And it's great value too - every month you'll discover five or six original Bustle & Sew designs, for all levels of stitchers, not all of which will be made available later for individual purchase.

Techniques include…

- Hand and freestyle machine embroidery
- Quilting
- Applique
- Softies
- Bags

And many other projects for your home and family.

The magazine also offers vintage patterns, projects from guest designers, features and articles about all the topics as well as extra information to help you with your own projects.

You can learn more about the magazine and subscribe on the Bustle & Sew website. But I believe that there's no substitute to seeing something for yourself, so you below there's a link to a selection of pages from my February 2013 issue. .

Just click here to download

And if you like it, then please do

visit my site to learn more and subscribe

www.bustleandsew.com/magazine

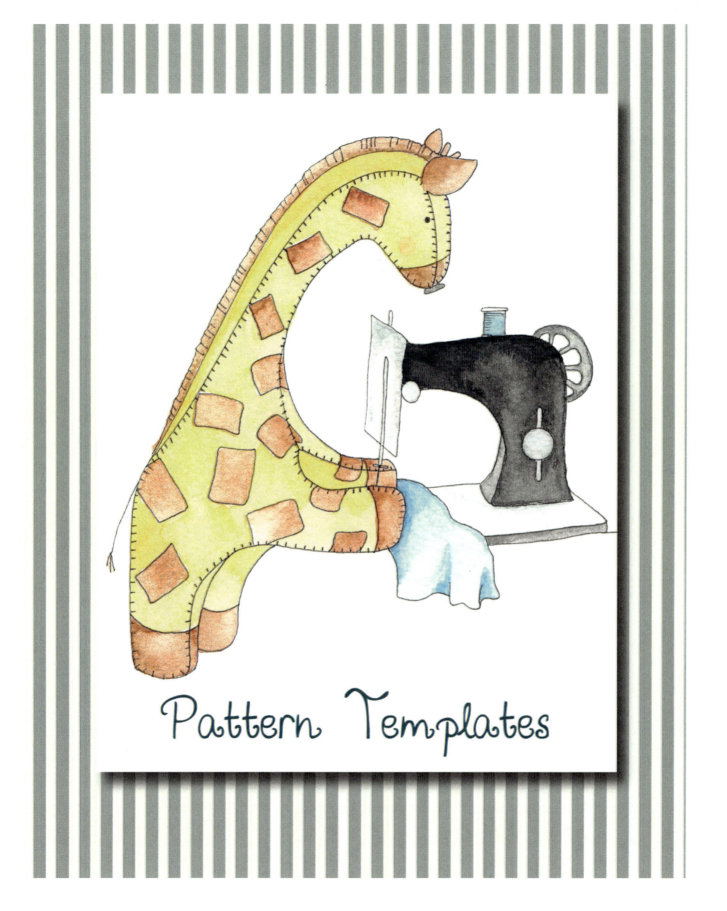

Pin Cushion Mice (page 12)

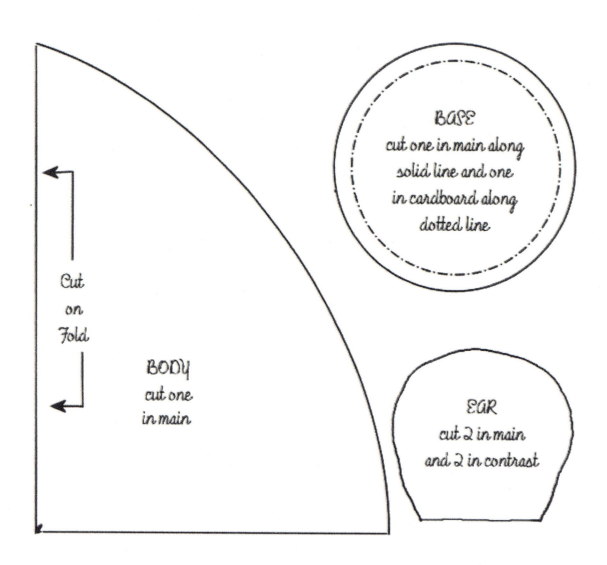

Seam allowances are included. Templates are actual size.

Two French Hens (page 14)

Template s actual size

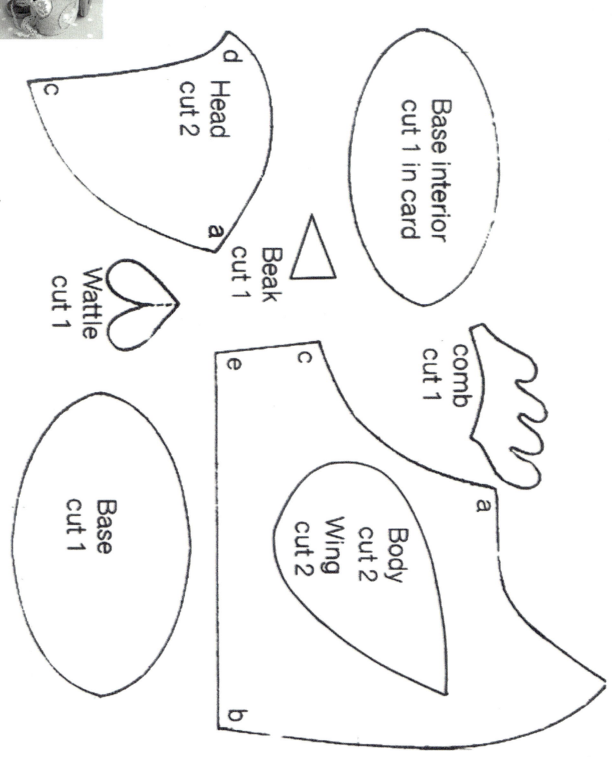

A Muddle of Bunnies (page 16)

Templates actual size

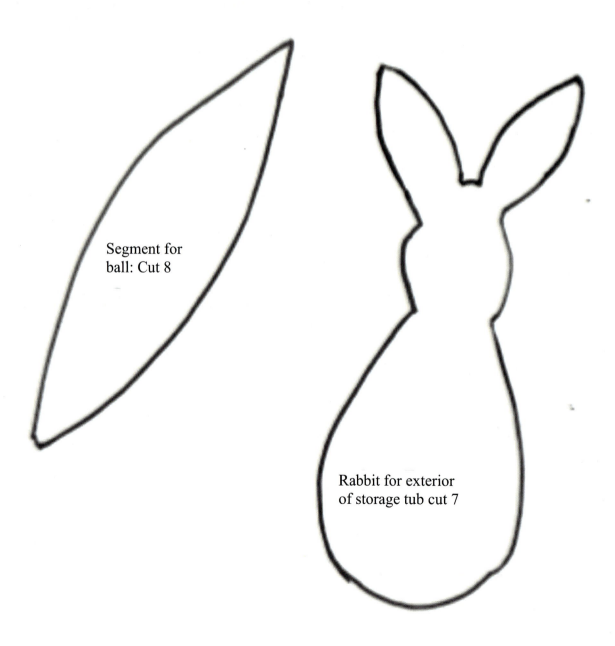

Segment for ball: Cut 8

Rabbit for exterior of storage tub cut 7

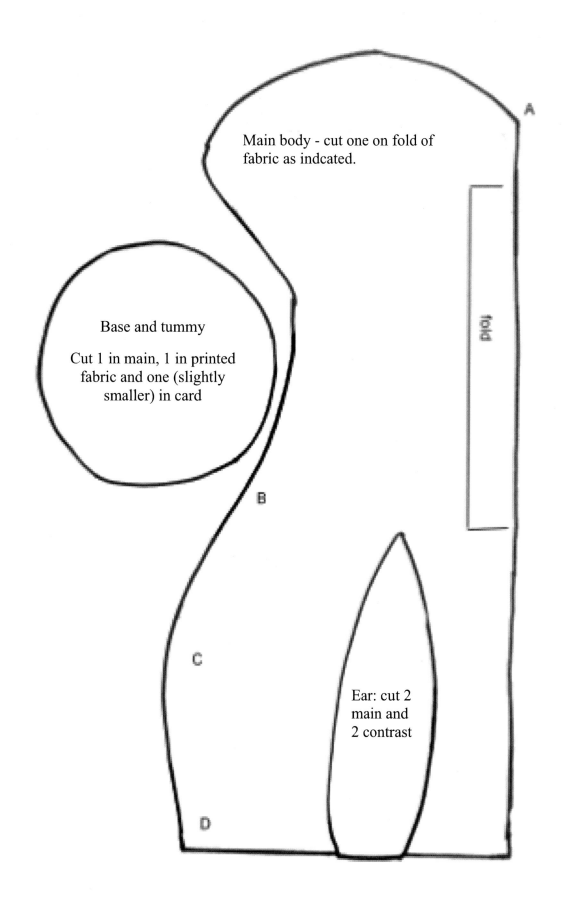

Flying Pigs (page 20)

Templates actual size

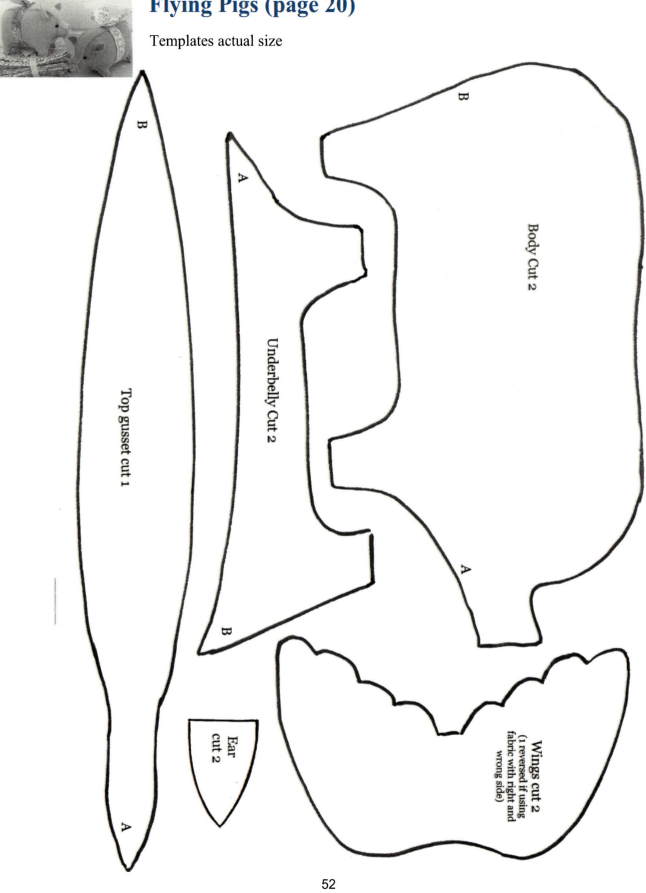

Hodge & Podge (page 23)

Templates actual size

Podge

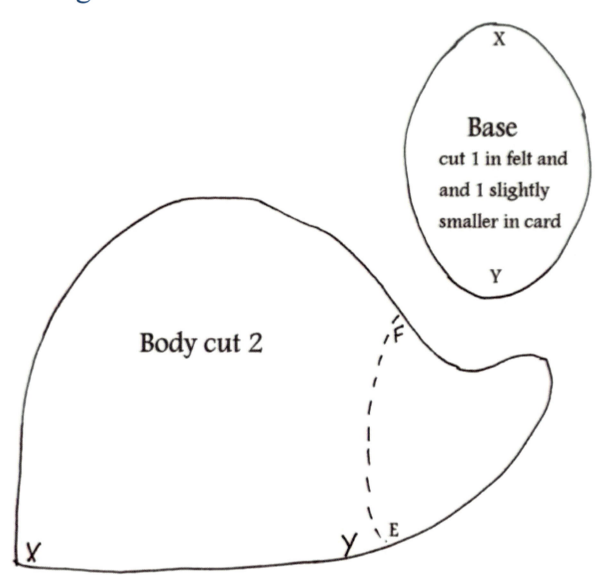

Base cut 1 in felt and and 1 slightly smaller in card

Body cut 2

Hodge

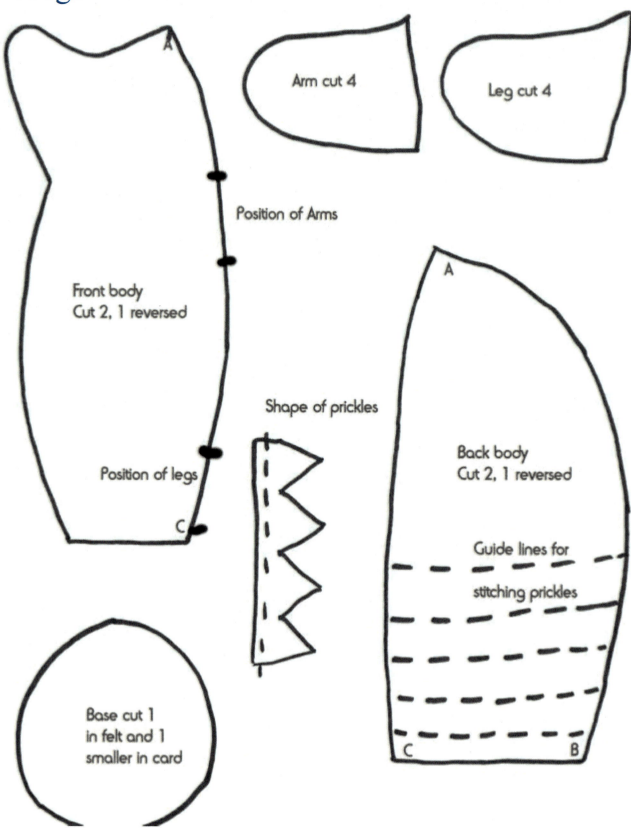

Fuzzy and his carrot (page 26)

Templates actual size

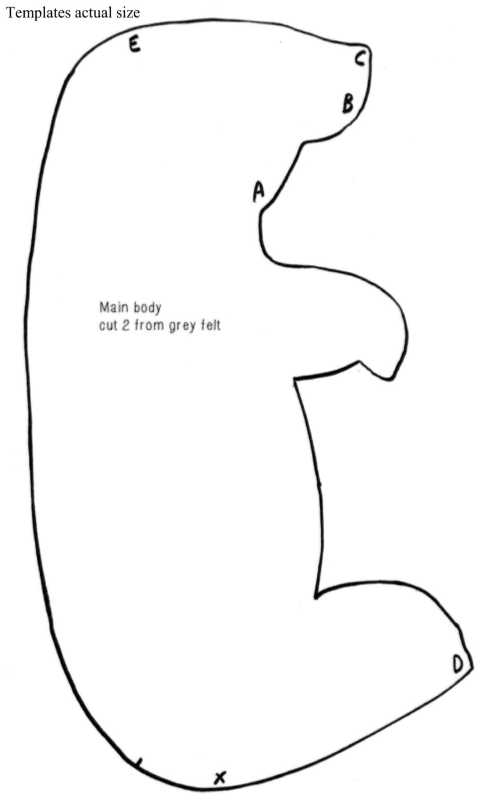

Main body
cut 2 from grey felt

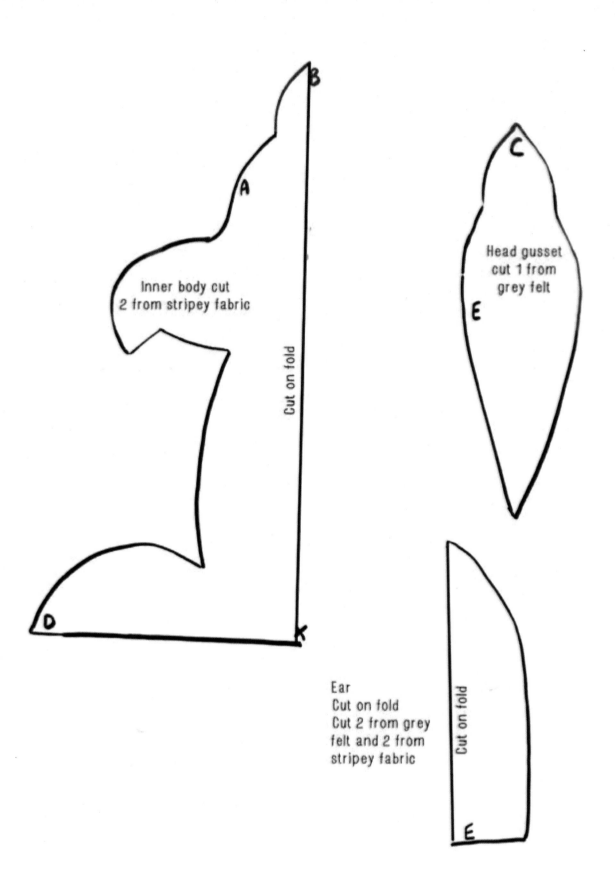

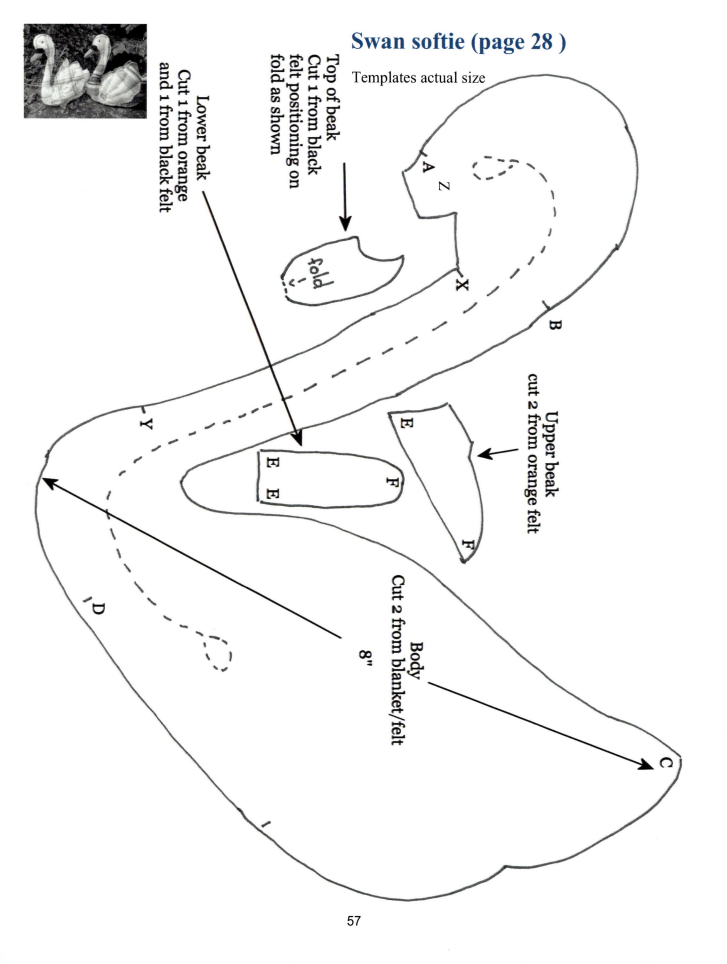

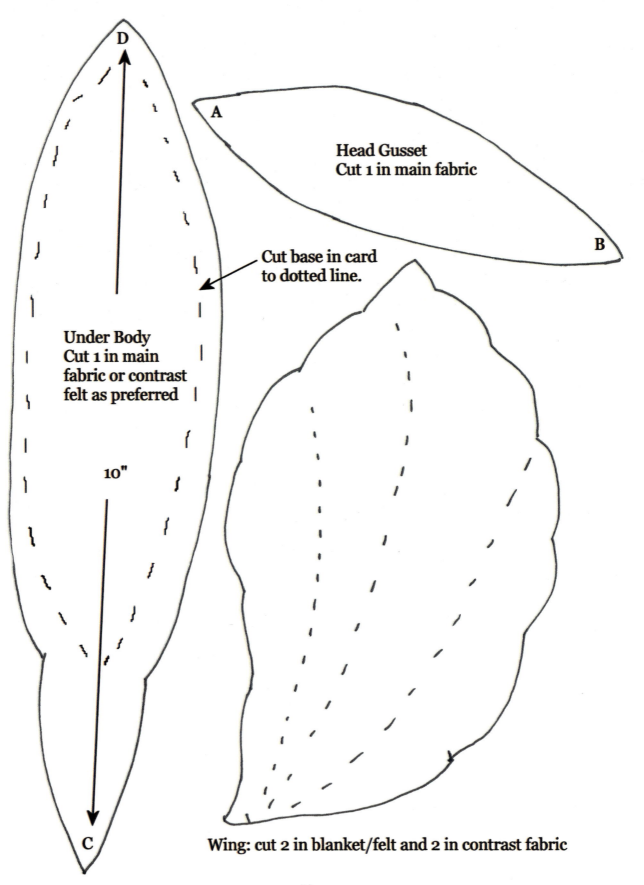

Deer Head (page)

Templates 75% of actual size. Increase by 130% on photocopier.

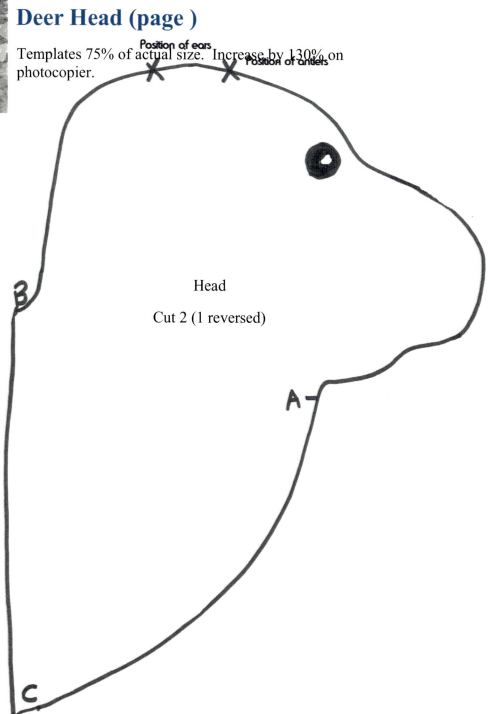

Position of ears
Position of antlers

Head

Cut 2 (1 reversed)

A

B

C

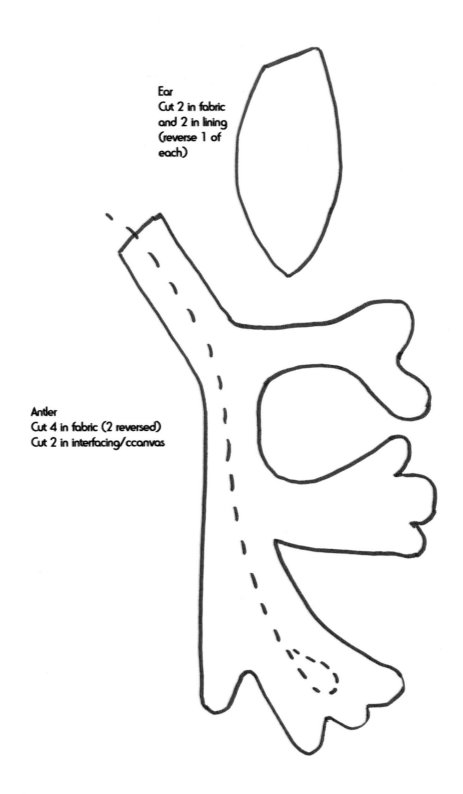

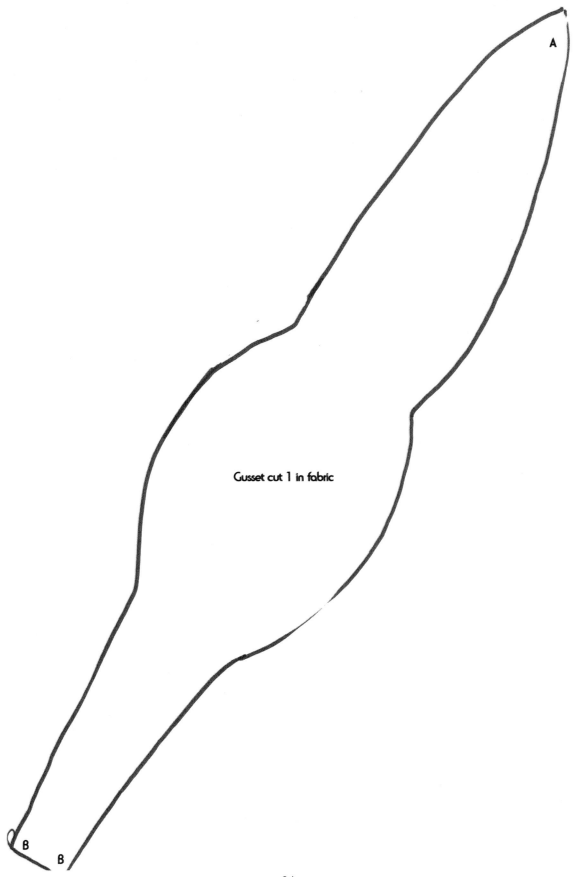

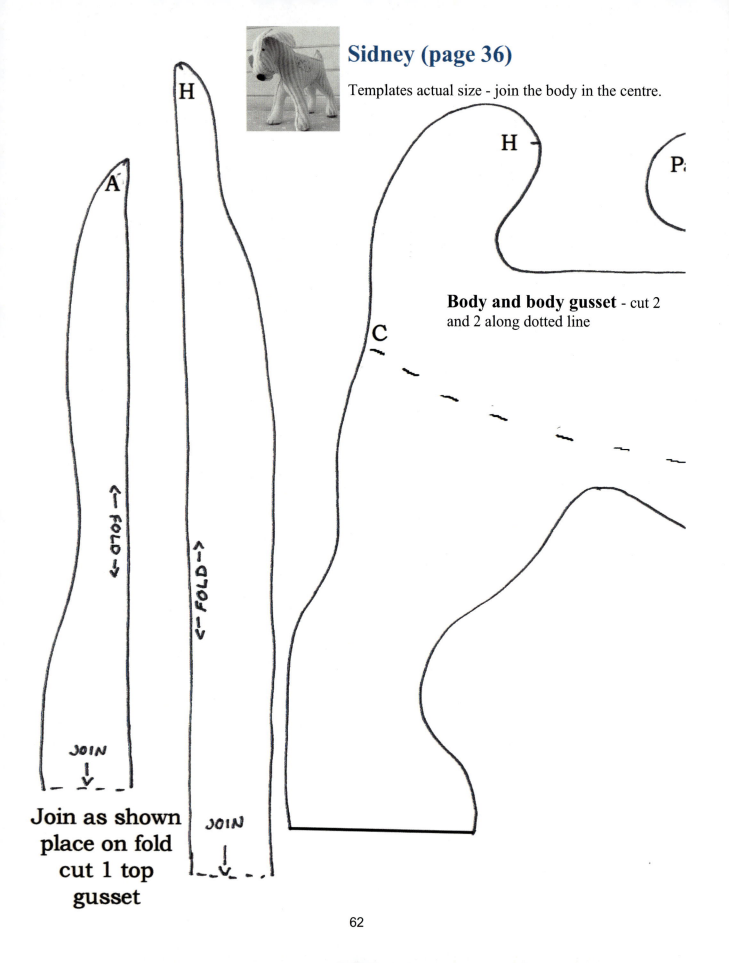

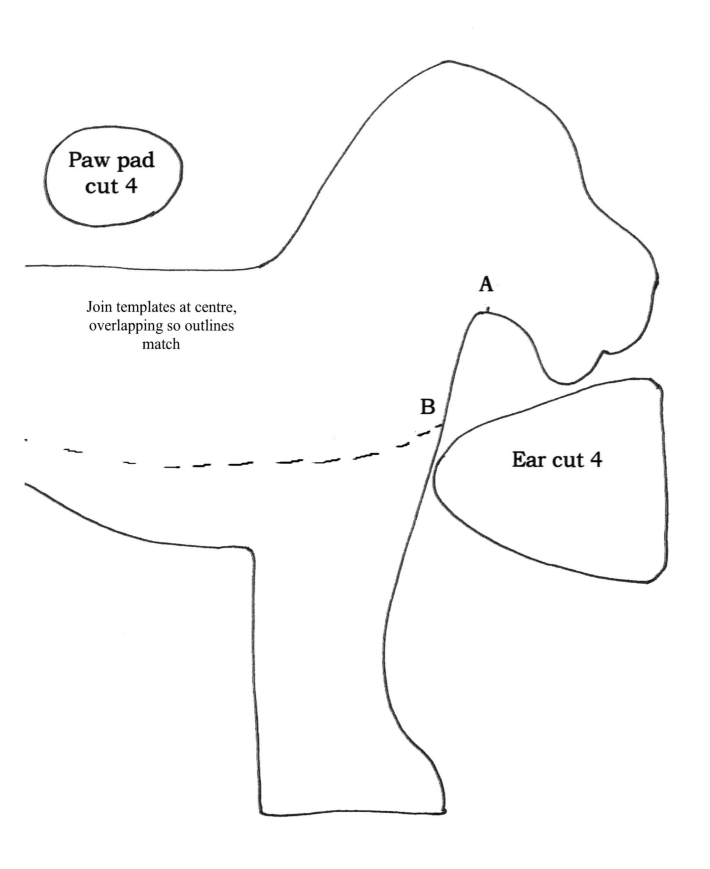

Brave Aviator Mouse (page 38)

Templates actual size

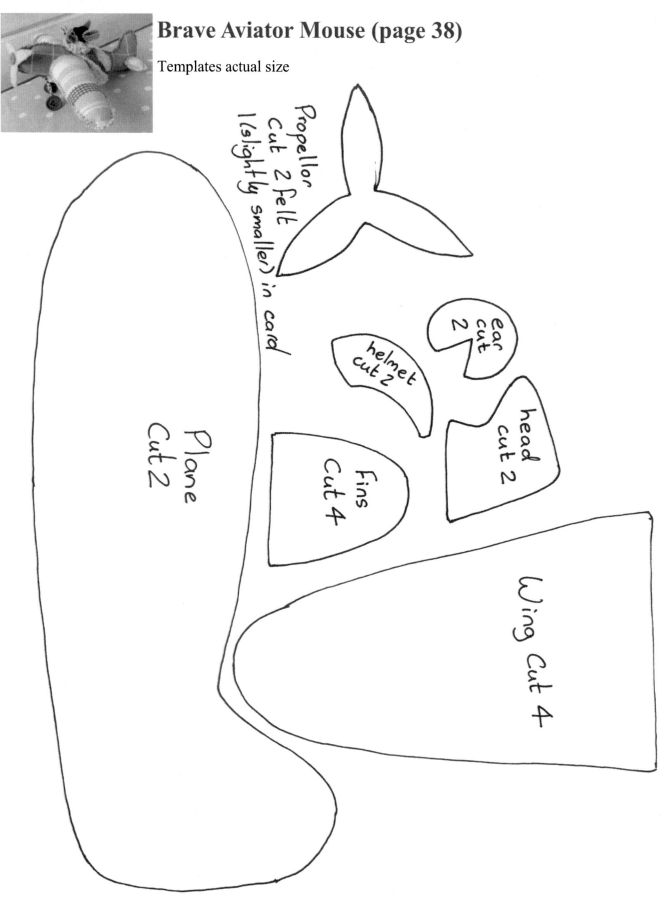

Little Giraffe (page 40)

Templates actual size

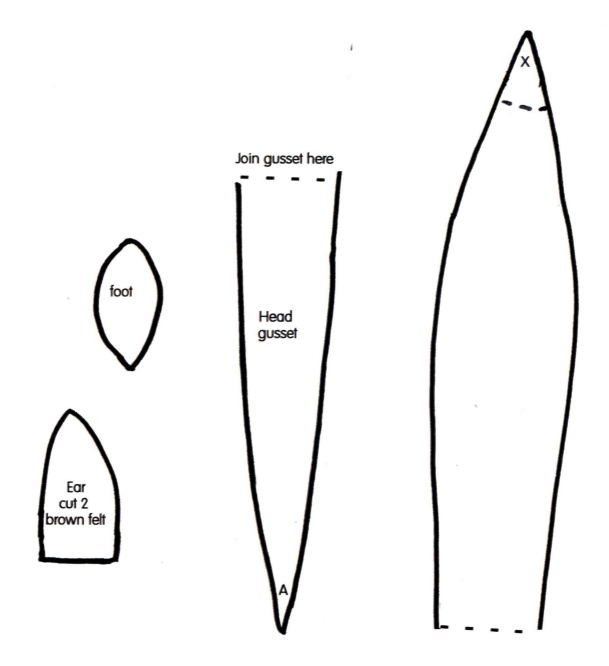

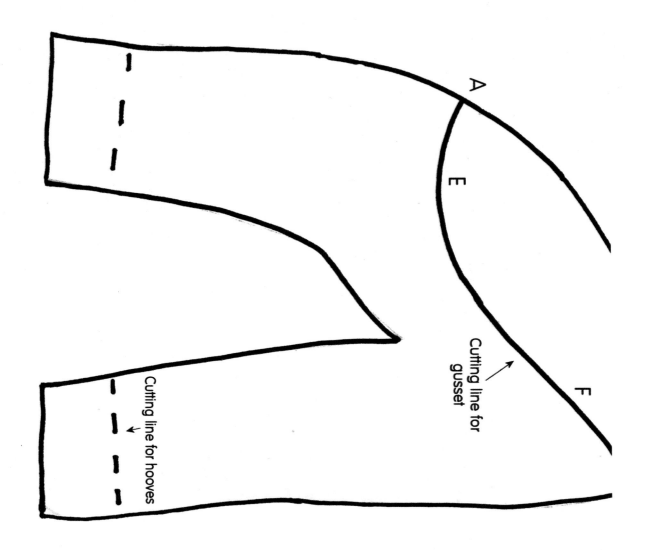

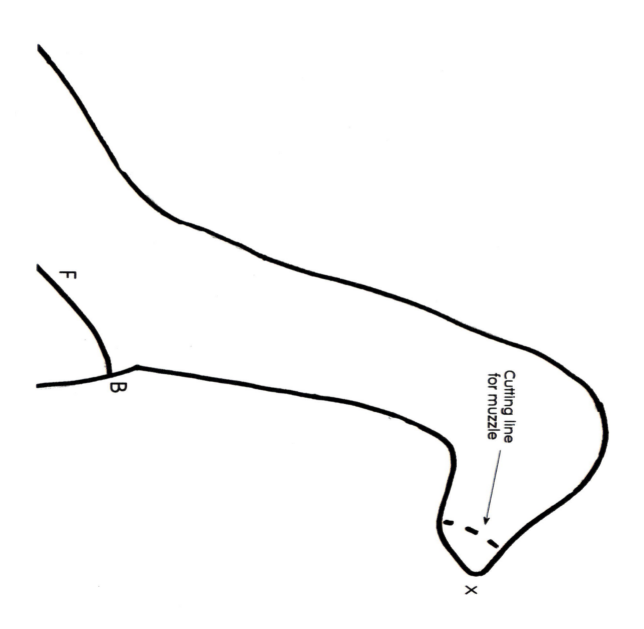

Fabric Fox Head (page 43)

Templates actual size

Head gusset - join at dotted line and cut one in fox red felt

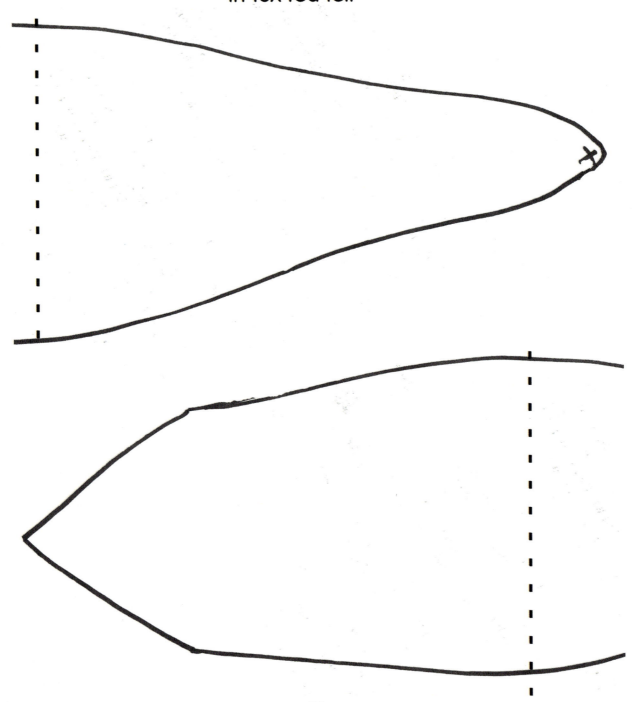

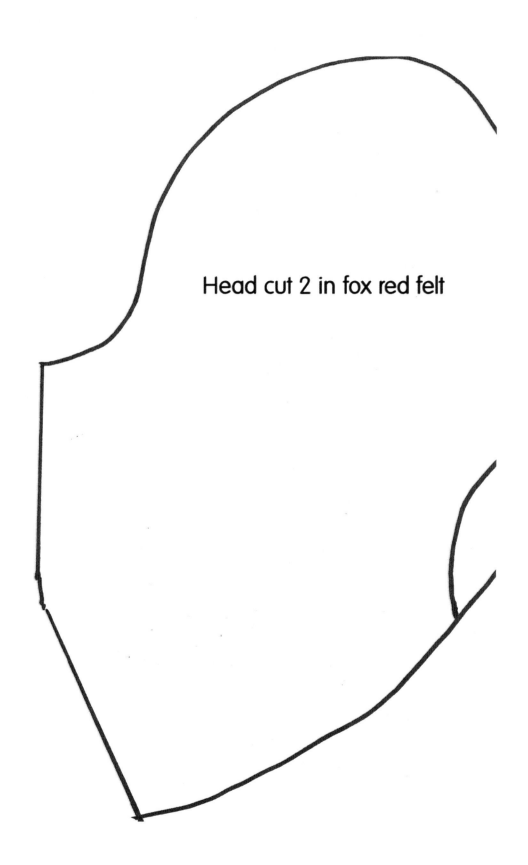

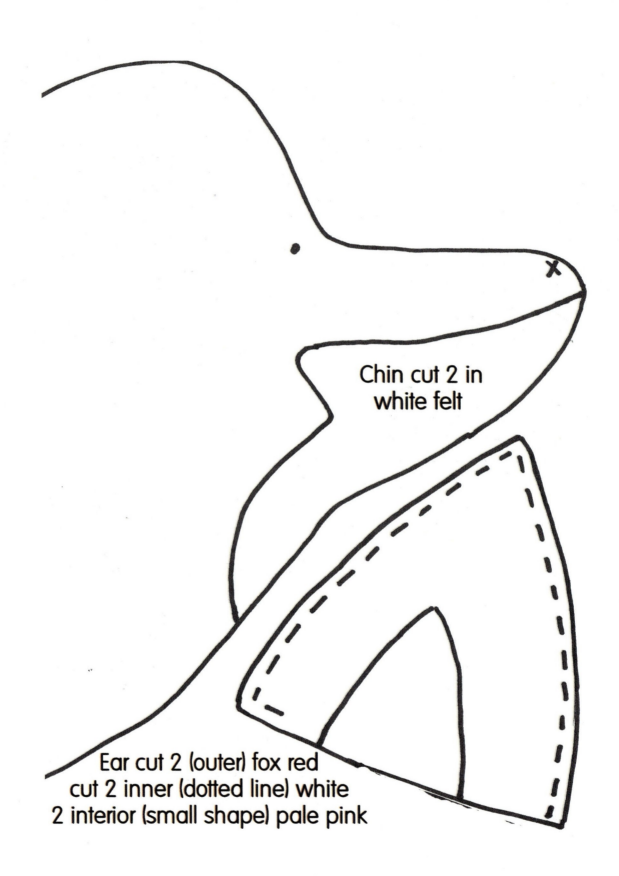

The softie illustrations inside this book are by my amazingly talented friend - and professional illustrator - Jacqui Bignell. I think she's illustrated each stitch wonderfully - and hope you like them too.

You can learn more about Jacqui and her online business Flapdoodle Designs over on her Facebook page - she'd love you to visit and say "hello!"

www.facebook.com/flapdoodledesigns

Jacqui has also designed some beautifully simple embroidery patterns - great for newbie stitchers - for Bustle & Sew.

www.bustleandsew.com

Find Bustle & Sew on Facebook too!

www.facebook.com/bustleandsew

Made in the USA
Las Vegas, NV
19 December 2021

38727342R00043